FOR MY DAUGHTER

_____

You're not a child anymore. You're growing up, and I'm so proud
of the woman I see you becoming. I don't always say the things
I hope and feel and pray for you, but as you read this book,
please know that these words come from a father's heart.
They come from my heart . . . for you.

LOVE,

_____

DATE

_____

Look for more places to write to your daughter on pages 37 & 60.

Listen, my daughter, to a father's instruction;
pay attention and gain understanding.

—PROVERBS 4:1

A Woman in the Making

GUIDANCE FROM A FATHER'S HEART

LANCE WUBBELS

Illustrations by C. MICHAEL DUDASH

COUNTRYMAN

Nashville, Tennessee
WWW.JCOUNTRYMAN.COM

Published by J. Countryman®, a division of Thomas Nelson, Inc.,
Nashville, Tennessee 37214

Unless otherwise indicated, all Scripture quotations in this book
are from The New International Version of the Bible (NIV)
© 1984 by the International Bible Society. Used by permission
of Zondervan Bible Publishers.

Other Scripture references are from the following source:

J. B. Phillips: The New Testament in Modern English, Revised
Edition (PHILLIPS). © J. B. Phillips 1958, 1960, 1972. Used by
permission of Macmillan Publishing Co., Inc.

J. Countryman® is a trademark of Thomas Nelson, Inc.
Project Editor: Kathy Baker
Designed by Koechel Peterson & Associates, Inc., Minneapolis, MN.
All illustrations are copyrighted and used by agreement with
C. Michael Dudash (www.cmdudash.com).

ISBN 1-4041-0020-2
Printed and bound in Colombia
www.jcountryman.com
www.thomasnelson.com

CONTENTS

Know That I Love You

One is not born, but rather becomes, a woman.
—SIMONE DE BEAUVOIR

A Father's Heart

WHEN MY DAUGHTER WAS A NEW-BORN, IT WAS MARVELOUS TO SEE MY FATHER HOLD HER. He would cradle her in his arms, and his steady blue eyes shined with a look I guess I'd forgotten—endless pools of love and gentleness and patience. That tender gaze for his granddaughter was stunning . . . beautiful . . . and a striking reminder that my father also loved me just like that.

My daughter has graduated from college and is away from home now, and I hope she's not forgotten, as I had with my father, that I love her with every fiber of my being. As was true of my father—and most fathers— I tended to feel more than I showed. I often failed to share the concerns of my heart for her. Sometimes, when I tried, the words fell far short of what I wanted to say, and the hugs were more awkward than comforting.

Young woman in the making, take the words in this book as reflections from a father's heart . . . as true of any father's loving heart . . . as true of your own father's heart. Perhaps your father is like me and just needs some help in saying what he really feels. May you find in these words the guidance, comfort, and love he has for you.

You Changed My Life

THERE NEVER WAS A DAY LIKE THE DAY YOU WERE BORN. Never was a moment when time so fully stood still. Never was before . . . never will be again. One moment with you changed my life . . . forever.

The first glimpse of your sweet face took my breath away, and I've never fully regained it. You were a miracle of dainty beauty, so soft and heaven fresh. It only took a second for you to become my little love and the joy of my heart. You will always be my treasure.

I remember the moment you first dawned on me. I was young, and I thought about how one day I would marry and have children of my own. I dreamed about you then . . . what you'd be like. I imagined you in my arms and how it would feel to call you my own. The truth is, you've been in my mind, sweetheart, for the longest time.

God put you in my heart long before you were conceived.

What a grand thing, to be loved! What a grander thing, to love!
—VICTOR HUGO

How beautiful is youth! how bright it gleams
With its illusions, aspirations, dreams!
—HENRY WADSWORTH LONGFELLOW

A Woman in the Making

IF THE EYES OF YOUR SOUL COULD PEER INTO MINE, YOU WOULD GLIMPSE THE DEPTHS OF MY LOVE FOR YOU. So precious and adoring, you made it so easy for me to fall in love. I delight in you! I rejoice in you! At times my heart aches for you.

I see before you a wide ocean of possibilities, and my prayers rise with the coming tides. There will be times of boundless imaginations and bright hopes and wonderful days that hold great mystery and beauty. And there also will come times of heartbreaking disappointments and extreme passions surging to life and extraordinarily difficult situations that will feel like the most frightening journey of a lifetime.

You are a woman in the making, my daughter, created to live life full of confidence and peace and joy. From childhood to amazing womanhood . . . there is nothing simple about the rite of passage. You are in preparation, getting ready to make your place in the world, and it does not happen overnight. You can get there . . . you can turn your dreams into reality . . . and I promise to always be here to help you fulfill them.

ADVICE ABOUT

Your Inner Self

A WOMAN IN THE MAKING

Above all else, guard your heart, for it is the wellspring of life.

—PROVERBS 4:23

Guard Your Heart

THE SOUND OF YOUR VOICE IS LIKE SWEET CHORDS TO MY EARS, AND YOUR LAUGHTER IS MORE ENCHANTING THAN THE MOST RAPTUROUS MUSIC I'VE EVER HEARD. Something about you is wonderful beyond measure . . . something fashioned and shaped by the divine. Only the God of love could have created someone as splendid as you.

I desperately desire the very best for you in life, and I hope that through the years you sense the wonder taking place inside you. As you grow and mature, who you really are is being shaped, your character is being molded, and it all is happening in the secret of your heart. Through the choices you make every day, you have the opportunity to build truth and beauty and love into your character and to keep out selfishness and lies and deceit.

You'll find that your heart is especially fragile during these years; it is vulnerable and easily influenced, both positively and negatively. My prayer is that you will be wise and guard your heart. Some of your friends will tell you that what you do doesn't matter. You'll face overwhelming pressure to conform to what others say and do. Listen to your conscience. Taking a stand for what is right and refusing to go along with a friend who is pulling you in the wrong direction is never easy, but it is a first step to becoming a woman of character.

BEWARE OF SHIMMERING IMAGES

THE FIRST TIME I HELD YOU, I FELT IN A DAZE THAT YOU WERE MINE . . . ALL MINE. And you are still mine, always will be mine, but I've had to share you with the world around us. Which concerns me—a lot.

I brought you into a world that is driven by subtle yet powerful lies. Here's one lie you'll hear over and over again: Success is measured by beauty, athleticism, popularity, academics, career, and wealth. A quick glance at the magazines at the grocery checkout counter defines those messages. Not only will these lies shout for your attention, but you'll feel pressured to spend all your time and energies in pursuit of them. And once you start the chase, you'll find that no matter how close you come to measuring up, it's never enough.

Don't buy into the lies, sweetheart. The values that society glamorizes are merely shimmering images draped over empty shells. Don't be deceived into chasing after hollow promises. Instead, take a look down your life's road and ask our Father in heaven what kind of a woman He wants you to become . . . and how you can become that woman. He made you, He loves you, and He wants the very best for your life. If you ask Him, He'll help you choose the values that will shape your character for a lifetime.

Youth is the time when one's whole life is entangled in a web of identity, in a perpetual maze of seeking and finding, of passion and of disillusion . . .
—ELLEN GLASGOW

YOU DETERMINE YOUR CHARACTER

How many times, I wonder, in the stillness of the night, have I stroked your hair and kissed your cheek? How many times have your whispers been heard by me alone? And how many times have I prayed for wisdom to raise you complete?

I have one word of wisdom for you that I treasure above all: You alone determine the person you will become, and it all comes down to who you are on the inside. Character is not a gift I can give you on your fourteenth or sixteenth or eighteenth birthday. Personal character is established and built over long periods of time. Your mother and I have tried to provide you with values to live by and standards for right and wrong, and your friends, teachers, and society also have a real and profound influence upon your thoughts and actions. But you decide what your character will become.

At school and within your own circle of friends, you have already seen what happens when people are careless about the development of their inner life. Like thistles and weeds, bad character thrives where there is no resistance. Issues of the heart that bring inner strength and confidence, such as the development of faith and purity, of truth and sincerity, of God's presence in your life, get smothered by the daily pressures to be popular or meet others' expectations. Don't let it ever happen to you, precious one. "Don't let the world squeeze you into its mold" (ROMANS 12:2, PHILLIPS).

Character builds slowly, but it can be torn down with incredible swiftness.
--FAITH BALDWIN

Be a Woman of Truth

Imagine how difficult it would be to go to a school where you could never believe anything you read or were told. You might even know someone who can look you straight in the eye and tell you a bold-faced lie, someone who thinks nothing of betraying your confidence. Since you were a young girl, I have tried to teach you that the truthfulness of one's character is the cornerstone for all of your relationships. If you fail to build truth into your life, it will result in serious consequences for the woman you will become.

People look for the truth in many different places today, places that are often misleading. So where does the truth begin? My precious daughter, it begins with a Person: Jesus Christ. He said, "I am the way and the truth and the life" (John 14:6). Truth begins in God, and without Him there is no basis for truth. As you grow in your relationship with Him in truth, He will change you more and more into a humble, grace-filled, loving person like He is.

Nothing will beautify your life as much as living every day by His truth. To walk in truth in all that you say and do will reflect a courage and dignity born from a clear conscience and clean heart. A heart that has a sincere commitment to truth is more precious than all the treasures the world can offer. Truth is a solid foundation that will not give way when temptation and trouble strike. Your choice to live by God's truth will make you a person who can always be trusted, a person worthy of loving friendships.

You will never find yourself until you face the truth.

—Pearl Bailey

Sow a thought, and you reap an act. Sow an act, and you reap a habit. Sow a habit, and you reap a character. Sow a character, and you reap a destiny.

—Anonymous

Pattern Your Life After Jesus

I'VE CELEBRATED MANY OF THE FIRSTS IN YOUR LIFE AND DELIGHTED IN EVERY STEP OF YOUR GROWTH. The steps toward becoming a woman who loves God, though, always begin in the heart and are not as easily noticed. In my life it started the day I realized that God loved me . . . totally loved me . . . and wanted the best for me. To experience His love changed my life. It became crystal clear that beyond anything else I do, there is nothing higher or better than to love and obey God.

I need to be honest with you: Loving and obeying Him will often mean a struggle. To do what's right, to do what God wants you to do, may cut into your fun and pleasure—but it will build the finest character in your life. When I went my own way, selfishness wove its way into the very fabric of my character. I did selfish things, and selfishness ruled my heart and wrecked my relationships. It subtly changed my thinking, hardened my heart, overpowered my conscience, and shut me out from the presence of God.

You'll find real joy, lasting joy, the joy of God, in a lifestyle that God commends. You'll never find joy or happiness by comparing yourself to others around you, especially your friends. But if you pattern your life to Jesus Christ, if you make it your heart's ambition to be like Him, you will find a peace and rest that nothing can take away.

Aspire to Great Things

YOU ARE PRECIOUS, AND YOUR LIFE IS A PRECIOUS GIFT FROM GOD. Tell yourself that every day, no matter how you feel, for it is the absolute truth. You are unique in all of God's creation, and He meant it that way. There has never been another you . . . and there never will be. With the natural gifts God has given you, only you will be able to do what you can do or in the way you can do it. You were given the gift of life by God to be all that He created you to be. In His eyes—and in mine—you are very special and have a vital purpose to fulfill in His world.

All the dreams you have ever longed for in life also are precious. Your heavenly Father sees the high goal that you aspire to attain, and He is there to encourage you to reach for it. He knows all that you yearn to be—something so great that nothing can banish it from your heart until it becomes yours. Take those dreams and nourish and protect them, for only you can make them real. Allow God to breathe His divine inspiration into your dreams. If you do, they will fill you with a passion to enjoy life to its fullest.

Remember that the person you dream of becoming also must include what you do in your life. The values you bring into your life will become the solid foundation for whatever you do. So weave into the tapestry of your life love, joy, peace, patience, kindness, and goodness. Without these qualities, any hopes you have of becoming the best you can be will remain only a dream.

Dreams are the touchstones of our character.
—HENRY THOREAU

Use your imagination not to scare yourself to death but to inspire yourself to life. —ADELE BROOKMAN

Go for Your Dreams

REMEMBER HOW YOU FELT WHEN A DREAM THAT SEEMED IMPOSSIBLE BECAME TRUE IN YOUR LIFE? You were thrilled! And as your father, my eyes filled with tears of joy for you. My love, you must never let your dreams die . . . for the death of a dream will only cause you to sink back into yourself. All your time and energy will become focused on self-seeking interests that will only twist you into a smaller and smaller person and make you miserable. That would break my heart.

I know some of your dreams have presented you with great obstacles. But don't give up on them just because they are difficult. Your path to success in life will begin the moment you lay hold of those dreams and pursue them with your whole heart. Allow those dreams to become a driving force to build your inner character. Let them be goals that motivate you to rise up and attain.

Go for your dreams and cast all fear aside. Never give up! Do something every day to make your dreams come true. Stay true to your values even if that commitment costs you dearly. To compromise will only bring temporary gain, not eternal. Be patient, and God will reward you openly.

Did you know that God also has dreams for you? Dreams to use you to accomplish His good purposes in this world in ways that will bring joy to those around you. And in the process you will be surprised by joy, and you will find fulfillment in your life that you never imagined possible.

ADVICE ABOUT

Your Outward Self

A WOMAN IN THE MAKING

Honor the Beauty Within

THE WORLD YOU ARE GROWING UP IN IS CONSTANTLY DRIVEN BY THE TRENDS AND LOOKS OF CELEBRITIES FROM HOLLYWOOD STARS TO SUPER MODELS. And the standard for beauty is confusingly reset on a daily basis. You already feel phenomenal pressure from all sides to try to conform to that standard as much as possible in order to be accepted. And it is only intensified by the constant spotlight of the media. They would have you believe that outward beauty is everything.

As difficult as it may seem, sweetheart, it is crucial that you come to terms with how you view beauty. Your evaluation of your own appearance will be a major factor in determining your self-esteem. If you follow the world's standards, you'll soon find yourself on a slippery slope. Very few people have the "right" face or the "perfect" body of the models splashed on the covers of fashion magazines. It is impossible for most to keep up—depressingly impossible. For many girls the pursuit of beauty becomes a never-ending chase.

Listen: Real beauty comes from within. There is a moral and spiritual quality shining from the heart that graces the most ordinary face with beauty. Happiness can flood the soul and transcend outward appearances. The beauty of a woman whose faith has made her a partaker of the very nature of God excels all other beauties. Outward beauty, when seen in this purer light, pales into nothing. What you are in reality, you are in soul.

Outside show is a poor substitute for inner worth.

—AESOP

To seek after beauty as an end is a wild goose chase, because it is to misunderstand the very nature of beauty, which is the normal condition of a thing being as it should be.
—JUDITH STOUGHTON

Realize the Nature of Beauty

EVERY WOMAN LONGS TO BE BEAUTIFUL. Billions of dollars are spent in the elusive pursuit of just the right look in our society. I hear your friends talk about appearances constantly when they are with you, yet their own definitions of what is truly attractive vary from week to week, from movie to movie.

To some degree we are all ruled by prejudice when it comes to appearance. We all tend to see faces, not hearts; body shapes, not personalities. I hope you never draw your conclusions about people only by what you see on the outside. You must realize in your heart that appearances can be extremely distorting. The most outwardly beautiful person may also be a very cruel or petty person, totally devoid of true beauty.

How refreshing it would be if above the world's declaration of beauty you could always hear the gentle whisper of true wisdom: "Man looks at the outward appearance but the LORD looks at the heart" (I SAMUEL 16:7). Allow your heart to embrace the wondrous truth and believe it with all your heart. God made you beautiful just the way you are! True beauty, you see, is an inner beauty of the soul. True greatness is greatness of heart. All that the world proclaims as outward beauty may fade away, but be assured that the qualities of your inner soul may continue to grow in beauty and worth.

Shine from the Inside Out

IF I COULD GIVE YOU ONE SPECIAL GIFT IT WOULD BE THE ABILITY TO LOOK IN THE MIRROR AND TRULY BE COMFORTABLE WITH HOW YOU LOOK. It is a marvelous quality that gives you a depth of inner strength to draw upon when the world issues a new style and bids you to pursue it. Being comfortable with how you look brings true liberation to your soul. Never let others determine or upset your personal convictions of what is beautiful and attractive. Above all else, pursue godliness in your heart, which is true beauty. Then follow your own inner sense of beauty as you make choices to adorn your outward appearance.

The day-to-day choices about makeup and the styles of clothes you wear are important. Both are used as powerful tools to communicate with people around us, whether you intend to send those messages or not. How you adorn your body will often be interpreted or "misinterpreted" as to what you are like on the inside. And people will respond to you by their perceptions. So always take care how you present yourself. Don't give anyone the opportunity to misjudge who you really are by the way you dress.

John Keats once wrote: "A thing of beauty is a joy forever." May your beauty be eternal.

OTHER GIFTS I'D LIKE TO GIVE YOU

_____

_____

_____

_____

The tragedy of our time is not that we are so ego centered,

so appearance besotted.

The tragedy is that we do not know what we like

until we are told by our advertisers and entertainers.

—JESSAMYN WEST

ADVICE ABOUT
Your Relationships

A WOMAN IN THE MAKING

Truth Lasts a Lifetime

YOU HAVE ALREADY NOTICED THIS WITH YOUR FRIENDS: NOTHING MAKES SOMEONE MORE UNATTRACTIVE THAN THE LACK OF TRUTH IN A PERSON'S LIFE. Lies and half-truths, no matter what the excuse, are deadly poisons that paralyze the soul. Very often a person will go to great lengths to devise them in order to avoid the painful consequences of a wrong choice. Or they are used to manipulate others' impressions.

Jesus said that when you "know the truth, the truth will set you free" (JOHN 8:31–32). The truth frees you from all the masks of falsehood and the damage that it brings. When lies are cloaked with the appearance of truth, others are deceived and hurt.

Confidence is shattered, and the breach of trust oftentimes is extremely hard to repair. It takes time to build a relationship in truth, but one lie can spoil any relationship.

"Buy the truth," wrote King Solomon, "and do not sell it" (PROVERBS 23:23), for truth is priceless. If others play deceiving games with you, refuse to join them. May the words you speak and the promises you make always be true. May your heart be free of deception, and may honesty be the hallmark of your life. As you journey through life, never give people a reason to doubt you. If you build your character on truth, my precious one, it will last a lifetime and even beyond time.

You cannot weave truth on a loom of lies.

—Suzette Haden Elgin

TREASURE YOUR TRUE FRIENDS

OF ALL THINGS MOST VALUED, MOST CHERISHED, AND MOST VITAL TO ENJOY IN THIS LIFE IS THE GIFT OF FRIENDSHIP. A true friend is that special person you have opened your heart to and allowed to peer inside and know you . . . really know you . . . and who has allowed you to look inside their heart and life with no walls to hide behind. A friend is someone who accepts you just the way you are, not the way they'd like you to be. No matter what life brings your way, a true friend will be there for you.

I've found that a good friendship never diminishes, even when distance and years separate you. The bond of love forged out of honesty and mutual respect remains vibrant and alive, always anticipating that moment to be reunited once again. All the dreams and hopes you once shared, the joys and sorrows known and carried together, those loving words spoken and tucked in your heart as treasures—time cannot tarnish.

But remember, sweetheart, friendships can also be harmful. The apostle Paul warns: "Do not be misled: 'Bad company corrupts good character' " (1 CORINTHIANS 15:33). Your choice of friends is incredibly important, for it will be a clear indicator of your inner character. If you hang out with the wrong crowd, you will soon discover that the moral stain of their bad attitudes and actions will overshadow yours, and the corruption of your heart is inevitable. If you refuse to pursue relationships that tear you down, you will never have a moment of regret!

True friends are those who really know you but love you anyway.
—EDNA BUCHANAN

YOU ARE THE KEY

You have some friends who strengthen you and challenge you to be the best you can be in whatever path life takes you. And when you stumble and fall, they are there to pick you up and encourage you to persevere. They are true friends, and it thrills me to see you with them. You are good for them, and they are good for you.

The key to great friendships begins with you, my love. If you're a friend to someone, honor and respect your friend at all times. Guard your relationships carefully. Clear up any misunderstandings as soon as they happen, and have nothing to do with petty attitudes of possessiveness and jealousy. They will creep in and slowly erode the trust you have taken so long to build. In the end bad attitudes will destroy even the best of friendships.

So once you find true friends, always be faithful to them. Set aside your wishes and take an interest in the details of their lives. Reach out to them and be genuine with them. Remember to be sensitive to their feelings. A little bit of kindness and a good sense of humor go a long way. If you devote yourself to being a true friend to others, you will reap one of the sweetest joys in this life. God will honor your integrity and reward you with enough kindness and love to make your heart run over with joy.

"My friends are my estate," wrote Emily Dickinson. May yours be vast and rich.

A friend gives us confidence for life, a friend makes us outdo ourselves.
—Anna Lindsay

In real love you want the other person's good.

In romantic love you want the other person. —Margaret Anderson

Love Is a Beautiful Gift

I TREASURE THE WONDERFUL CAPACITY I SEE THAT YOU HAVE TO LOVE. My heart's desire is that someday you will find a fine young man—a true soul mate—whom you can love with all your heart. The journey to that great gift of marriage will not be without temptations along the way. Today, many brides have given their love away so many times that it's difficult to know what remains of their hearts.

You are surrounded by a stream of lies about romantic relationships, and I pray for you to have the courage and strength to meet each challenge that comes your way. The world will constantly try to weaken your holy standards and impose its own immoral ones. From books to movies to television to sex education classes, the world has redefined romance and love as only sex—intimate encounters that are natural and fun, with no morality at stake. "Be careful for your own protection," the mantra goes, "but if it feels good, do it." Do not listen to these lies.

The desires you feel to love someone intimately are a part of God's design for your life. But those desires are a sacred, beautiful gift that you must preserve and allow to grow and develop within His loving boundaries. Trust Him to bring you to womanhood with a maturity that reflects the grace and beauty He has bestowed on you. True romance should be reserved for that special time when both you and your husband are ready to embark on that journey of marriage with all of its responsibilities and joys.

Gertrude loved with all the delusion of romance, and, like many a young enthusiast, had mistaken her imagination for her mind.
—SUSAN FERRIER

Take a Long Look Ahead

SWEETHEART, THERE'S NO REASON TO RUSH INTO RELATIONSHIPS WITH BOYS. Needing a boyfriend to make you happy or to look cool puts you in a dangerous position. And though it might sound like a long way off, if you wait to develop a serious relationship until you're eighteen or twenty, you will be much wiser in your decisions, and you will spare yourself a lot of trouble.

Enjoy your friendships with boys, but always remember what I have told you. These feelings that ebb and flow like the ocean's tide are undeveloped and have little to do with true love. Guard your heart closely and allow yourself to grow into the person God wants you to be. Take a long look ahead to your wedding day. You must decide who you want to be and whom you want to marry. Have you set character and spiritual qualifications that you will not compromise? The gift of love and intimacy you want to present your husband on that special day must be wrapped in the choices you make today. Above all else, save yourself totally—physically and emotionally— so that someday you can give yourself without reserve or regret.

My father's heart whispers the ancient wisdom: Save yourself for your husband—heart, soul, and body. And until that wondrous day arrives, continue in the integrity of those high standards. It will establish you and win you respect for who you are. Finding the right person to spend your life with is not about a popularity contest—it's about your life.

ADVICE ABOUT

Your Spiritual Self

A WOMAN IN THE MAKING

You Were Made for God

MY HEART FOR YOU IS BUT A GLIMMER OF GOD THE FATHER'S HEART FOR YOU. He is real and He is personal. He created you and me to enjoy His world and to love Him. As part of His creation, we are here because He is here, and we can only make sense of our lives in a meaningful relationship to Him. Faith begins the moment we accept Him as He is—that He is God, our God, and that He waits lovingly for us to respond to Him with our love.

Some people view faith as an embarrassment or a crutch for the weak, which is unfortunate for them. Faith, when it is vital and real, always beautifies a person's life. It always brings confidence to one's personality, an inner power and strength from God, and joy and love. It becomes the inner dynamic that will empower you to be who you really are. Your personal faith in God will enable you to move forward with courage when crossing mountains of adversity or taking new steps in your life.

There was a time when I was foolish enough to think I could be satisfied with the things the world has to offer. I had no idea that God created my heart to never be complete or fulfilled until I possessed a living faith in Him. No wonder I was so restless and unhappy. And what a relief to discover that God had placed within me a desire to know Him, to find pleasure in Him, that was truly satisfied through a relationship with Him. Incredibly, you and I were made for God, and He delights in us.

To have faith is to have wings.
—JAMES M. BARRIE

Without faith, nothing is possible. With it, nothing is impossible.
—MARY McLeod Bethune

Trust & Follow Jesus

I CAN'T IMAGINE ANYONE WHO LOVES TO BE WITH YOU MORE, TO HOLD YOU TIGHT, AND TO LOOK INTO YOUR EYES THAN ME. But that's what God is like, that's how He loves us, and that's why our faith in Him changes us from the inside out. It naturally draws us into prayer, to talking with God and discovering His thoughts toward us. And that's why it's so easy, if we have disobeyed Him, to tell Him we're sorry, to confess our sins and be cleansed in our hearts. God even sends the Holy Spirit to fill our hearts, restoring peace to a guilty conscience and calming fears with His presence.

I hope you've seen in my life that God is more than church statements about Him. Jesus Christ is more than a wonderful Christmas love story. Faith is not something you and I create on our own. It is the opening of the eyes of our soul to the person and majesty of God as our Father. It is the fixing of trust in Jesus Christ as the One who gave His life to save us from our sins, who rose from the dead as the Lord of life, and who calls you and me to love and follow Him.

There is absolutely no life that compares to one following Jesus Christ. There is nothing more charming or daring or adventurous than a life whose reflection is Him. I see that charm in your life, and it's truly beautiful.

Let Jesus Purify Your Heart

WHEN IT COMES TO THE DEVELOPMENT OF A GODLY CHARACTER, JESUS CHRIST WAS CLEAR ABOUT THE GREATEST PROBLEM WE WILL HAVE TO FACE: "For out of the heart come evil thoughts, murder, adultery, sexual immorality, theft, false testimony, slander" (MATTHEW 15:19). The enemy lies within our very own heart.

Over the years I've discovered that all my efforts to change myself are useless . . . and oftentimes painful. Even in my greatest attempts to free myself, deep down I knew something was wrong inside my heart. Jesus said that those who long for true freedom must allow Him to make their hearts pure. Unless the inner life is renewed by the divine, our thoughts, words, and actions will never be clean.

You may wonder if your heart truly could be "purified." With all my heart I tell you YES. "If we confess our sins, He is faithful and just and will forgive us our sins and purify us from all unrighteousness. . . . and the blood of Jesus, His Son, purifies us from all sin" (1 JOHN 1:9, 7).

You will never think, say, or do anything that cannot be washed away. You can be "white as snow" (ISAIAH 1:18). You can be made completely new inside, but only Jesus' death on Calvary's cross can give you this freedom from your sins. His death is of infinite value, because He who never sinned gave Himself as a sacrifice in your place. He alone can make and keep you pure within. It is but one simple prayer to make it your own.

DEAR GOD,

I ADMIT THAT I AM A SINNER.

I KNOW I'M LOST WITHOUT YOU. PLEASE FORGIVE MY SINS.

COME LIVE IN MY HEART. I'VE MESSED UP BEFORE,

AND I KNOW I'LL MESS UP AGAIN, BUT THANK YOU

FOR ALWAYS BEING MY TRUE FRIEND.

WITH THE HELP OF THE HOLY SPIRIT, I'LL KEEP STRIVING

EVERY DAY TO BE A TRUE FRIEND TO YOU ALL MY LIFE.

IN JESUS' NAME.

AMEN.

Blessed are the pure in heart, for they will see God.

—JESUS CHRIST (MATTHEW 5:8)

Strive to Be Holy

I WISH YOU COULD SEE YOURSELF AS I SEE YOU . . . THE WOMAN YOU ARE BECOMING. I wish you could feel in your heart . . . even for a second . . . what I feel for you. If you knew the source of joy you are to me, you would be overwhelmed.

My prayer for you every day is that you long for the beauty and inner strength that comes to a young woman who has given her heart to God. The transformation that takes place when you love God and delight in His ways is truly something to behold. To be free from the condemnation of sin and its crippling effects in your life is marvelous. But to possess an abiding peacefulness, a quiet confidence, a never-ending joyfulness . . . and a love that has its springs in God—not perfect yet, but refreshingly pure—is God's awesome gift.

To be a daughter of God is to know and love Him above all else as your heavenly Father. It means to have a pure heart adorned with a quiet, humble dignity that is incomparable in excellence. And I see that in you, my precious one. It is both charming and disarming—the beauty of an untainted spirit. It shines with a divine purity not dimmed by the world's pretensions. It is the seed of nobility that, if nourished, will crown your life with the most honorable title of virtuous distinction—a woman of God.

The serene beauty of a holy life is the most powerful influence in the world next to the power of God. —BLAISE PASCAL

BE STILL AND KNOW

As your father, I'm concerned at how crazy your life seems to be. I see you continuously on the run, pushing to keep up, always having something else to get done. And as you mature into a young woman, you'll find yourself juggling a career, family responsibilities, hobbies, and public duties. There'll never be enough time, money, and breaks from life's pressures.

But in the midst of all this turmoil and noise, God is speaking to you, "Be still, and know that I am God" (Psalm 46:10). Can you hear Him? Have you ever stopped to listen? Do you believe that He is with you, right now—literally, with you? I can assure you that He wants to be your truest Friend and that He wants to spend time with you. The Lord is asking you to quiet yourself, to sit at His feet and listen to Him.

I see that thirst you have in your heart to know God. Take the time to get alone with Him, for only His presence will fulfill that desire. He longs for you . . . waits for you to come to Him with all your heart's dreams. He knows that many of the concerns you are trying to deal with will vanish when you know and experience Him as your heavenly Father. He is not far off, but is right there with you. He wants to meet your deepest needs. The yearning within you will only be satisfied when you find God, and He cannot be found in the midst of noise and restlessness.

Prayer enlarges the heart until it is capable of containing God's gift of Himself.

—Mother Teresa

MAKE GOD THE LOVE OF YOUR LIFE

DEAR ONE, GET ALONE AND QUIET YOUR SOUL. LEARN TO LOVE THE SILENCE, FOR IT IS IN SOLITUDE WITH GOD WHERE YOU LEARN TO DEPEND ON HIM ALONE. Reflect upon the wondrous person of God. Open His timeless Book and hear His gentle voice speaking to you. His Word will breathe life into you, and His truths will be inscribed on your heart. God will not rest until you know Him as your best friend. He will pursue you relentlessly until He is the love of your life, because He knows that He is the answer to all the needs you have.

Even Jesus Christ regularly sought times of reflective solitude with the heavenly Father. His life demonstrated the tremendous value of prayer. Make it, my daughter, a pattern for your life as well. You can talk with God, tell Him of your joys and hopes and desires, and receive back His answers to your own heart. In prayer God comes to us and calms our fears, gives us His perspective on our lives, fills us with peace and rest, and grants us understanding of the things that please Him. In those quiet times He comforts us in His loving arms and touches us with His grace.

Though you may feel all the pressures of the world, you cannot afford to miss out on time for God. Give Him the chance to be your God and to do all that He says He'll do for you. He has promised to lead you beside still waters, to give you rest in green pastures, and to restore your soul. He makes certain that nothing in heaven or hell can separate you from His love. The choice is yours. Will you make His friendship a priority in your life?

God is the friend of silence.
—MOTHER TERESA

A PRAYER FOR

My Daughter

_____, there's no way I can tell you
all the things I've prayed for you over the years,
but this prayer is a tiny part of what my heart holds for you.
I love you.

_____

_____

_____

_____

_____

Fathers can only give their daughters two lasting bequests: one is roots, the other is wings.